Plan Your Dream
Destination Wedding
In Weeks

Plan Your Dream Destination Wedding In Weeks

Contents

Introduction

You may not be a professional wedding planner. Perhaps the thought of organizing your own wedding feels as novel and confusing as it is exciting. Yet, as you hold this book, something about the idea of arranging a destination wedding really captivates you. You might have heard stories of other people's destination weddings. Perhaps you think such weddings are expensive affairs meant only for the rich. Or that they are out of your reach due to lack of time or other resources. Or perhaps you'd love to plan a destination wedding but don't know where to begin. This book is designed to equip you with the practical knowledge necessary to plan your destination wedding and more importantly – enjoy the process.

Organizing a wedding in a short time can be ambitious, and even more so if arranged from a distance. But don't let that put you off! A lot can be achieved quickly if you know exactly what to do. The secret to planning a destination wedding well and in a short time is smarter planning – this book shows you how. Together, we can plan your dream destination wedding by following some guidelines step by step.

The word 'wedding' had always conjured up images of sunny locations amidst nature for me. So when my boyfriend proposed around springtime, I immediately envisioned getting married in a warm outdoors place by the sea. But I didn't want to wait a whole year to get married in the summer. Then it hit me – we had less than 3 months to arrange our wedding in a different country to make my dream a reality!

We started searching immediately for a location based on our wedding vision and budget. It was a hectic few weeks but we finally found the perfect venue on the Greek island of Corfu. Interestingly, all the advice we found was targeted towards planning weddings at least a year in advance. People who heard about the limited time we had were pretty skeptical about us pulling it off. Moreover, we had never been to Greece! As time was limited and we both had busy lives, we had to quickly figure out the most efficient ways to organize our wedding.

In the end, our wedding turned out to be an unforgettable experience for all. Guests remarked that it was the best wedding they had ever been part of! Following this, I started to help friends plan their own weddings in various countries. Over the years, I have witnessed a wide variety of weddings, including extremely well-organized ones. These experiences have helped me figure out how to plan weddings efficiently. I'd like to share what I have learned so you can have your dream wedding too.

This book illustrates how your destination wedding planning journey might unfold and visualizes the flow of decisions you need to make. A destination wedding has its own unique challenges. Researching your options takes much longer and you may encounter language barriers. However, a DIY wedding does not mean a less glamorous wedding! Don't worry if you feel that you have very limited time or a tight budget — I will help you to realize your ideal wedding vision by guiding you through the precise steps you need to take. We will start by sorting out key aspects such as the budget, location, venue, date, guest numbers and then move on to decisions like ceremony details, decorations and the reception menu. I share snippets of my own experience so you can see your own wedding materialize through my story.

Planning a wedding is like solving a puzzle — there are lots of pieces to fit together. Each chapter in this book is like a puzzle piece that you need to put together to complete the entire wedding plan. I truly hope that this book will be a source of encouragement to you to organize your own amazing destination wedding!

How To Use This Book

There's something magical about getting married to your beloved in a far-away location. This book presents a clear practical guide to help you organize your own destination wedding. It demonstrates smart and efficient wedding planning practices and ways to save time and money. Whether you wish to arrange your own wedding or ask a wedding planner to help you, the ideas in this book should help you plan better. Additionally, the principles laid out here can be applied to local weddings as well.

The chapters in this book are arranged in the order that they should be planned but this could change depending on your own requirements. The book is organized in several themes. Chapters 1 through 8 discuss how to get your wedding fundamentals sorted. These topics are central to your wedding planning and should be completed first. At this stage, you can communicate your intention to get married to others and start estimating how many people might attend. Once you reserve your venue, you can book your accommodation and transportation and buy wedding insurance if needed, as described in Chapters 9–11. You can then proceed to send out final invites to guests (Chapter 12).

Chapters 13–17 reveal the importance of carefully selecting your bridesmaids and groomsmen and organizing your wedding attire, hair and makeup and rings. Wedding ceremony-specific information, photography and videography as well as decorations are discussed in Chapters 18–22. Chapters 23–26 are related to the wedding reception and describe how to arrange catering and entertainment. Gifts and favors are discussed in Chapters 27–29. Chapters 30–31 show how to conduct wedding rehearsals and plan the wedding day's activities. Finally, Chapters 32–35 revolve around post-wedding activities like cleaning up and planning your honeymoon. You can dive into chapters as and when you need to. The idea is to use the questions and my experiences to reflect on what you would like for yourselves.

There are tips throughout the book to help speed up planning and save money. In each chapter, a useful tip is highlighted to plan a successful wedding and avoid some common pitfalls. Checklists and infographics are included to help you keep track of important information and provide valuable insights. Make notes or fill in the relevant fields, even if it's with approximate information to start with.

Arranging a wedding may make one feel overwhelmed, especially due to the plethora of choices. One needs to be realistic about organizing a destination wedding, especially if time is short. Sticking to a clear plan is vital to organizing everything from a distance and in good time. This book will arm you with down-to-earth advice and ideas that are easy to implement, making planning easier and much more fun to tackle. An example timeline to arrange a destination wedding in 3-6 months is included but you may have a different timeline for yourself. I planned my own destination wedding in less than three months and so can you!

Wedding Planning Timeline

3-6 MONTHS BEFORE

decide wedding style

set budget

choose country

get marriage license

decide date

make guest list

send Save the Dates

reserve venue

book officiant

reserve accommodation

arrange transportation

get insurance

send invites

select wedding party

buy wedding attire

2-3 MONTHS BEFORE

choose wedding party attire

find makeup artist & hairstylist

buy rings

plan ceremony

book photographer & videographer

book caterer

choose cake

1-2 MONTHS BEFORE

buy decorations

find florist

book entertainment

write speeches

purchase favors & gifts

decide wedding day's timeline

plan day after

pack

have final dress fitting

book honeymoon

have hair & makeup trials

have wedding rehearsal

THE BIG DAY

get married!

Your Wedding Vision

Decide your wedding style by imagining your ideal wedding to identify elements you love.

Why is it important?

Your wedding vision determines the ambiance of the big day. It also directly affects your wedding expenses. Every couple has their unique preferences when it comes to weddings. You have the power to make your wedding the most amazing and memorable experience of your life, so why not include elements you love?

Steps to take

A fun way to get your wedding planning started is by imagining what your dream wedding would look like with your partner over a meal. Write down 5 things that would be most important for you at a wedding. In particular, think about the elements you can't imagine your wedding without, the parts that would be nice to have and the bits that you wouldn't mind skipping in order to stay within your budget. This will save time at the planning stage as you'll know what to search for, something that is difficult to achieve from a distance.

Don't worry if it's not evident at the beginning — the more you reflect on these details, the clearer it will become. You can also check online or read magazines for inspiration. Envisaging your dream wedding is a gradual process and may take a few iterations to determine.

Questions to think about

* Would you like an indoors (e.g., palace or hotel) or outdoors (e.g., mountains, beaches, gardens, orchards or vineyards) wedding?

  _____

* Would you like your wedding in spring, summer, fall or winter?

  _____

* Would you like a grand wedding or an intimate affair?

  _____

* Would you like a traditional wedding or an unconventional one?

  _____

* Would you like a particular wedding theme or ambiance such as Hawaiian, retro, funky, Star Wars, etc., or none at all?

  _____

* Would you like bright colors, earthy tones, paler pastels, white, off-white, black or other seasonal colors for your wedding?

  _____

My experience

I kicked off our wedding planning by discussing my wedding vision with my partner. I'd always imagined having an outdoor summer wedding amidst nature with spectacular sea views. It would ideally be a relaxed event, filled with people closest to me and my partner. My partner's ideal wedding would be in a forest, filled with lots of games! As we explored our options for the wedding, we realized that there were certain things we both definitely didn't want while others just felt right. For instance, neither of us wanted any wedding speeches but we both wanted to have some shared experiences with guests before and after the wedding day. Although we didn't agree on everything, we ended up sharing an overall vision for our wedding.

Key takeaway

Deciding your wedding vision gives you a head start on the planning and helps you realize the key desires you have for this very special day. Doing this as the very first step is worth it as you are much more likely to transform your vision into reality. This is the first piece of the puzzle that you need to put in place for your dream wedding!

Budget Setting

Decide how much you'd like to spend on the wedding and the absolute maximum you can afford to spend – and don't deviate from the latter.

Why is it important?

Setting a wedding budget is crucial as expenses can quickly spiral out of control and lead to debt, which can be dangerous. Your budget will affect every aspect of your wedding – when and where you get married and the type of wedding itself. A destination wedding can be cheaper than a traditional wedding due to a potentially smaller guest list and combined wedding and honeymoon expenses. But don't rely on monetary gifts when deciding on the budget!

Steps to take

First, discuss with your partner about what you can both afford to spend, who will pay for what and your spending priorities. Keeping track of your outlays is key to spending within your budget. Use a budget tracker with various fields such as attire and catering. If you don't have a clue about expenses for a particular category, get quotes from multiple vendors and fill in the estimated amounts.

Adjust the budget on the next page based on what matters most to you. Multiply your total budget by your preferred percentage amounts to get each category's budget amount. Have a safety net (say, 15% of your total budget) for emergencies or in case priority items cost more than anticipated.

To reduce costs, communicate with venue managers and vendors via email or phone rather than flying in multiple times. Pay for services via debit cards to have proof of transactions and to track expenses or credit cards to have protection in case of disputes. Use services that charge negligible commission or fees for international transfers. If a vendor does not provide an invoice, note down any amounts paid with dates and request the vendor to sign this or confirm these in writing.

My Wedding Budget Breakdown

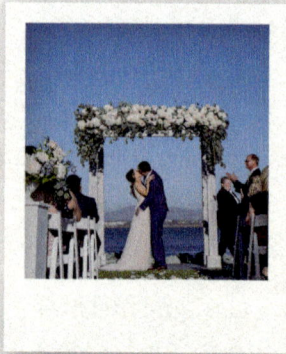

Total Budget
$25000

Actual Expense
$20100

Emergency Fund
$1000

Ceremony
$700 (3.48%)

Groom's Attire
$500 (2.49%)

Bride's Attire
$1200 (5.97%)

Accessories
$450 (2.24%)

Reception
$4000 (19.90%)

Food & Drink
Included

Photo/Video
$2500 (12.44%)

Rings
$900 (4.48%)

Hair & Makeup
$500 (2.49%)

Other Apparel
$150 (0.75%)

Cake
Included

Entertainment
$350 (1.74%)

Flowers & Décor
$250 (1.24%)

Accommodation
$1600 (7.96%)

Transportation
$5000 (24.88%)

Favors & Gifts
$150 (0.75%)

Stationery & Invitations
$0 (0%)

Honeymoon
$1700 (8.46%)

Wedding coordinator
$0 (0%)

Financial (insurance etc.)
$0 (0%)

Miscellaneous
$150 (0.75%)

To save, choose destinations with good foreign exchange rates, cut down on guest numbers, wedding party sizes and meal courses, offer limited alcohol, choose weekday dates, reuse ceremony flowers for the reception, buy cheaper rings, use local services at the destination and spend your honeymoon close to the wedding location.

Questions to think about

* How much can you afford to spend based on your and your partner's income and overall financial situation (savings, debt, parents' financial input, job security)?

* Who (bride, groom, family, bridesmaids, groomsmen, etc.) will pay for what?

* What non-negotiable items would you like to splurge on and what would you like to save on?

* Will your budget allow for inviting plus ones or families of friends?

* Do you need to buy dresses for your bridesmaids, groomsmen, altar boys and flower girls (the latter may be customary in some countries or cultures)?

* Will you incur any hidden extras such as taxes, service charges, tips, delivery and setup charges?

* Can you opt for local options at the destination and if yes, can you ask your venue to suggest trusted local service providers?

My experience

We decided to limit our wedding expenses to a year's savings. We managed to spend within this limit primarily due to the choice of location — a Greek venue was considerably cheaper than other shortlisted countries! Moreover, our venue was family-run and the hosts helped us to decrease our costs by contacting local vendors in Corfu on our behalf. Advice on service providers on online forums and social media groups from the local area helped reduce our expenses further. We limited decoration charges by making some decorations ourselves and minimized our entertainment expenditure by creating our own music playlists. I also managed to find an ex-display wedding dress which was heavily discounted. However, the alteration costs amounted to half the dress' price!

We didn't want to save on photography and videography, so we allocated a chunk of our budget to them. Some guests had asked us to book their accommodation and flights, especially if they would be sharing accommodation with other guests or if they found it difficult to find suitable places close to the venue. Unfortunately, we did not recover all these expenses and ended up with extra costs. In hindsight, we should have sent all guests a list of potential rental options and let them do the bookings themselves.

Fact Check: Average wedding costs are about $22,172 in the UK (Source: Hitched Survey 2022) and $28,000 in the US (Source: The Knot Study 2021).

Key takeaway

The wedding day is only one special day out of a lifetime of shared moments – it is better to make many more beautiful memories together rather than spend most of your money on one event. In the end, your marriage is the focus of the day and guests will remember a day filled with love and laughter and how they felt overall, rather than details like the color coordination of the ceremony background!

The Destination

Your destination will be inspired by your vision but should be practical with respect to budget, wedding regulations, transport and visas.

Why is it important?

Your destination will influence your wedding style and experience and should be carefully chosen after considering pros and cons.

Steps to take

Find potential destinations by using image searches online with keywords characterizing your dream wedding. Arrive at a decision on (a) country (b) city or area (c) venue type (d) venue. If your partner is from the destination country, ensure that his or her family also have to travel to the venue city or town to make it a special destination wedding experience for everyone.

Questions to think about

*   Does your dream destination involve any of the following: a place of worship, a secret city location, a glamorous hotel lounge, a sun-kissed beach, a venue surrounded by majestic mountains, a pretty garden or a lush rainforest?

*   How much time and hassle is required to fulfill the eligibility criteria to get married at the destination?

*   Do you have enough time to conduct the required administrative processes and abide by the destination laws for weddings (if having your legal wedding there)?

* How expensive is venue hire, vendor services and travel fares for the destination?

  _____

* Is the destination easily accessible?

  _____

* Is there sufficient availability of venues and accommodation options for guests?

  _____

* Do you or your guests need visas to visit the destination country?

  _____

My experience

I wanted a wedding close to a sun-kissed beach. So we searched for places with sunny weather and beautiful beaches in Europe. We ended up shortlisting Spain, Italy, Cyprus, Greece, France and Montenegro. We eliminated all but Italy, Cyprus and Greece after checking the local wedding laws. This was before we decided to have the civil wedding in the city where we lived. We emailed venues, asking for photos and prices of venue hire and catering. We were limited to places where an officiant would be willing to marry us outdoors, so we contacted officiants simultaneously.

Unfortunately, most Italian venues were quite pricey and so we focused on Greece. We were overwhelmed by the choice of islands and never having visited Greece, choosing a location was tough. We finally found a couple of officiants and were left with three locations: Corfu, Halkidiki and Cephalonia. The last two places were not easy to get to for guests and flights were pricier compared to Corfu. We thus chose Corfu and started to look for the most beautiful areas there.

Key takeaway

Choosing the right destination is key to ensuring that most people you want at your wedding can attend. Think about what you both want and make a list of must-haves to decide.

Letto il presente atto agli intervenuti con 'l'atto con noi sottoscritta

firma dello sposo   firma dei testimoni

The Marriage License

Depending on the destination's wedding laws and the time you have, having separate legal and social weddings might be easiest.

Why is it important?

Getting your marriage paperwork in order is vital to getting your status as a married couple legally recognized.

Steps to take

Although having a single ceremony is generally easier, separating the legal/civil and social ceremonies can be simpler if the paperwork requirements of the destination country are substantial or unachievable in a short time frame. Work out the requirements, timelines and deadlines for the administrative procedures for the destination country with your partner and plan things backwards in time for maximum efficiency. Documents required may be birth certificates, passports, divorce papers or death certificates of former spouses (if applicable) and certified copies of these documents.

Questions to think about

* Will your destination wedding be legally recognized?

   _____

   For a combined legal and social wedding at the destination:
* What are the residency criteria and documentation requirements for legal wedding ceremonies in the destination country?

   _____

* Do you have enough time to acquire the required documents?

   _____

* Do you need to translate, notarize or apostille (get government-issued certification) any documents?

---

* Can you travel to the destination country before the wedding to fulfill the local residency requirements?

---

* Does the destination country require any medical test results?

---

* Do you know someone who speaks the local language to verify that you have understood the local laws correctly?

For separate legal and social weddings in different countries:
* What paperwork is required in your country of residence?

---

* Do you have enough time to prepare documents for the official license?

---

* Do you have at least a few days between the legal and social ceremonies to ensure that there are no issues in having the

  marriage legally recognized?

---

* Do you have to send anyone (e.g., your officiant) proof of your legal marriage certificate before the social wedding?

My experience

We wanted to have a legally recognized wedding at the destination. However, after conducting some research, we realized that this could be quite problematic. Requirements to register weddings vary greatly across countries and differ between residents and non-residents. Our destination required several documents from embassies or consulates that would have been difficult to obtain in two months. Fortunately, we got the legal registration done in our country of residence, which was much easier. Our social wedding was held two weeks later in Greece.

Example requirements (these are subject to change) for non-residents to marry in top wedding destinations:

Destination	Residency	Main Documents Required
Italy	None	Photo ID, certified copies of birth certificates, declarations "atto notorio".
Mexico	3 days	Official ID and a copy, marriage license form, birth certificate, visitor's permit, blood tests, completed pre-nuptial course.
Thailand	None (need to complete paperwork at Embassy in Bangkok – ~2 days)	Valid passport and affidavit notarized by your Embassy or Consulate stating that you are both free to marry. All marriage paperwork must be sent translated into English and be authorized at the Thai Foreign Ministry.
Hawaii	None	Valid ID for age proof, get marriage license no earlier than 30 days before the wedding.
Greece	None	Passports, certified birth certificates, certificate of no impediment to the marriage issued within the last 3 months, announcements in a local Greek newspaper, certified translations of required documents.

Key takeaway

Although arranging the necessary marriage paperwork might be tedious, it is vital to ensure that it is done accurately and in good time.

Your Wedding Date

Ensure that the people you want most to attend your wedding can do so on your desired date and that the venue and officiant are available.

Why is it important?

Your wedding date may have an effect on the wedding ambiance due to the type of weather or proximity to holidays and also influence who can attend.

Steps to take

Decide the time of year first and then the date. Be flexible! Finalizing the date will depend on the kind of weather you prefer at the destination, who can attend and venue and officiant availability. Get better wedding deals at off-peak times like mid-week and seasons like spring and fall. A daytime reception may be cheaper than dinner.

Questions to think about

* What weather do you prefer – do you see yourself looking glorious among fresh spring flowers or bathed in warm sunshine or looking glamorous under thundery rain clouds or waltzing under falling golden autumn leaves or as a snow princess?

* Which month would you like to get married in and go on your honeymoon?

* Do you have a special date when you want to get married – your first date, the date of proposal, a birthday or any other date of significance?

* Are there any national holidays where you or most of your guests live that might drive up prices of flights etc., but enable you or your guests to enjoy an extended holiday?

_____

* Are there any days when your preferred venue is cheapest?

_____

* Would you like a sunrise, morning, afternoon, sunset, evening or night wedding?

_____

My experience

I'd always wanted a sunny wedding. To maximize the chances of this happening, we considered months between May and August for European summertime weather. I wanted to get married on the anniversary of our first date. But this was adjacent to a holiday weekend and this drove airfares up. Such fares would have been too much for some of our guests to afford. After avoiding clashes with other personal celebrations and exorbitantly priced dates, we settled upon a date in June after confirming the officiant's and the venue's availability.

Key takeaway

The climate in a particular season will depend on your destination — you could have a tropical wedding in February or a snowy wedding in July. The beauty of a destination wedding is that you can choose!

The Guest List

Inform the people who make you happiest as soon as possible about your preferred wedding date and destination.

Why is it important?

A guest list helps to ensure that everyone close to you is invited and enables you to keep track of the total headcount, while making sure that you don't invite more people than you can afford. It also assists with deciding the ceremony and reception seating plan.

Steps to take

Every wedding is unique. Whether you decide to invite 2–3 guests or 300+, just make sure you are comfortable with it. Due to the associated travel costs and effort of attending a destination wedding, only the people who really want to attend will come. Your expenses can inflate quickly if everyone you invite decides to attend. If you'd rather not invite certain people including those who invited you to their wedding, explain to them that it is an intimate affair.

Guests typically pay for their own trip. To help your guests have a relaxed time together, you can host a meal or activity for them before the wedding day. You can also consider thanking all your guests for making the trip with a welcome party or thank you note when they arrive. You can't satisfy everyone so do not change any dates or arrangements to fit your guests' needs.

Questions to think about

* Would you prefer a small close-knit affair or a grand celebration?

_____

* How will your budget affect your maximum guest headcount?

_____

* Whom do you absolutely want at your wedding?

_____

* Do you want to invite plus ones (serious relationships only?) and kids?

_____

* Do you wish to invite any of your colleagues or your manager?

_____

* Do you need to invite some people out of courtesy and to avoid hurting their feelings or because your family is pushing you to? If yes, are they likely to turn up especially if it requires financial and time commitments to attend a destination wedding?

_____

* Would you like to use phone calls, mails, emails or messenger services for invites and announcements?

_____

* Would you like to send an informal announcement first to get headcount estimates and send more formal Save the Date type of invites later?

_____

* Whom do you want to invite for events like rehearsal dinners?

_____

My experience

Creating the guest list was much trickier than expected! We first invited our immediate family members and closest friends. Some people weren't sure if they would get leave from work to attend but we had to book the venue anyway due to the tight timeline. We then invited other friends, colleagues we got along really well with and acquaintances who would be upset if not invited (not recommended!). We didn't leave anyone out based on how far they lived or their financial situation. We wanted to give them the opportunity to come at least – they could always refuse . We also wanted everyone to feel free to bring anyone they wanted, so plus ones and kids were very welcome.

However, the numbers rose quickly as many guests wanted to bring friends as plus-ones. But due to several guests canceling last minute, we ended up with 55 guests. We later became good friends with some of the guests' plus-ones! We communicated all wedding details via messaging services or phone calls and got quick informal responses most of the time.

Key takeaway

Filter people to share your special day with – invite those you treasure, people who fill your lives with joy and uplift you.

The Venue

Contact multiple venues simultaneously about hosting your wedding ceremony and reception using an email or phone message template.

Why is it important?

The choice of venue will influence every aspect of your wedding, from overall ambiance to costs and even the type of menu available. In many ways, the venue is even more important than the destination.

Steps to take

Find potential venues in the destination country online with keywords characterizing your dream wedding. Create an email or phone inquiry template and use a tool like mail merge (https://tinyurl.com/ycyr7ch6) to send several emails at once to the shortlisted venues. Follow up with them once if they don't reply. Ask someone to help you write inquiry emails in the local language if needed. Check if you can rent public spaces like parks and museums for minimal fees or for free.

Questions to think about

* Is your ideal venue a church, wedding hall, hotel, garden, orchard, restaurant, beach or any other non-traditional place?

   _____

* Can the venue accommodate your approximate guest headcount?

   _____

* Can you host your ceremony and reception at the same place to save on venue hire fees, transportation, décor, etc.?

   _____

* Which of these criteria will you use to shortlist venues: background scenery, all-inclusive venue and catering options, good transport options, local accommodation availability and costs, duration available, availability of features like rooftops and pools, entertainment options, proximity to nature, provision of rentals, on-site coordinator presence, parking, disabled access, reviews, and cancellation and refund policies?

_____

* Does the venue offer an all-inclusive accommodation package which includes a free wedding or a complimentary room for the wedding night?

_____

* Are there accessible toilet facilities and contingency rain or sun cover at the venue?

_____

* Will you encounter any external people like resort residents or have complete privacy at the venue?

_____

Example inquiry email and follow-up email (to negotiate ceremony and reception venue options and charges):

Dear Sir/Madam,

We would like to have a symbolic wedding ceremony and reception in Greece this summer, ideally in the first two weeks in June 2023. I was wondering if this would be possible at your venue for a party of around 60 people and how much this would cost? If yes, would it be possible to share some photos, 3D views or videos of potential ceremony areas (e.g., rose gardens or beaches) at your venue? Thank you very much in advance.

Looking forward to hearing from you.

Best regards,
Mona Lisa

Hello again,

Many thanks for your reply. Would it be possible to reserve the garden at your venue for the wedding ceremony and have a buffet reception afterwards? If yes, what would be the cost?

Many thanks and kind regards,
Mona Lisa

My experience

I searched online and contacted venues such as hotels, gardens and public spaces in our shortlisted countries via email. I asked about the possibility of hiring them for weddings, their availability on certain dates, guest capacity, reception options and prices for an estimated number of guests. Several venues had bespoke packages to suit a range of budgets. We were mainly looking for beautiful outdoors scenery, reasonable prices and good transport options.

Finding our dream wedding venue was nothing short of magical! I chanced upon a beautiful image of bougainvillea plants overlooking the sea while searching for venues in Corfu online. An image search revealed that it was from a family-run resort. Although their resort accommodation was sold out, the venue hostess graciously agreed to host our wedding. The venue had many picturesque areas and we chose a spot which overlooked the sea and mountains for our ceremony. We also picked an outdoors area near a shaded space for our reception in case of rain.

Key takeaway

Keep track of multiple venues using a spreadsheet to compare features like package types, hiring fees and availability on your preferred dates.

Venue Comparison Components

Venue hire fees

Date availability

Capacity

On-site accommodation availability

On-site support availability

Bad weather cover

Ceremony Officiant

Choose an officiant you feel comfortable with and who is willing to help you turn your wedding vision into reality.

Why is it important?

The wedding officiant is a person who can lead a legally recognized wedding ceremony. For religious weddings, the officiant should also be authorized by the relevant religious institution.

Steps to take

Discuss with your partner about the type of officiant you'd like before commencing your search. You may need to search for the officiant in parallel with the destination or venue.

Questions to think about

* What are the local laws regarding who can officiate weddings?

  _____

* Do you want a religious, professional, ordained friend or family member or a state-authorized civil officiant?

  _____

* Can you get names of officiants from local organizations like churches, councils and ceremony venues in shortlisted locations?

  _____

* Is the officiant willing to travel if needed to conduct the wedding ceremony?

  _____

* Do you need to arrange the officiant's journey to the venue and provide accommodation and travel expenses for the officiant and any assistants?

_____

* What requirements does the officiant have on the ceremony length, content, having original vows or readings, setting (outdoors vs indoors, non-religious site for a religious ceremony, necessity of permits, etc.) and provision of items like hymn books or candles?

_____

* Would you like to invite your officiant and any assistants or partner to the wedding reception?

_____

* Do you need two separate officiants for the legally recognized civil ceremony and for the social wedding, if they are separate events?

_____

My experience

We started searching for an officiant in our shortlisted countries before deciding on the final location as we needed someone willing to marry us outdoors in the destination country. In the end, we found a kind British priest, who was based in Corfu every summer, to officiate our wedding. We had a few video calls with him before the wedding so we could get to know each other better and this made the ceremony quite personal.

Key takeaway

Have regular conversations with your officiant at the planning stage to get to know each other better and ensure a smoother and more personal wedding experience.

Accommodation

Search for accommodation close to the wedding venue and send a list of accommodation options to guests after booking your own place.

Why is it important?

You may need to think about accommodation not just for yourselves but also for immediate family members, for before, during, and after the wedding day.

Steps to take

Determine with your partner the type of accommodation you'd like for your wedding night and where you will stay before and after the big day. Also, clarify who will pay for what before committing to booking accommodation for anyone else.

Questions to think about

* Would you like separate accommodation for you and your partner before the wedding day and share lodging with family or friends?

   _____

* Does the wedding venue have any accommodation available?

   _____

* How long do you need accommodation for?

   _____

* Do you need to book accommodation for your immediate family?

   _____

* Is there enough accommodation near the venue for all your guests during the wedding week?

   _____

* Is the available accommodation affordable for all your guests?

_____

* Would some people consider sharing accommodation?

_____

* Who will pay for guests' accommodation if you book?

_____

* Do you need to communicate your arrival times to the accommodation personnel in advance?

_____

My experience

We booked our accommodation for the days leading up to the wedding in various hotels and guest houses near the venue. Staying at different places helped us to experience slightly different areas of Corfu and accommodation types. This was feasible only because we traveled light and the accommodation choices were close to one another. We booked separate places for myself and my fiancé using online booking platforms to stay with our respective families before the wedding.

Several guests had asked us to book their accommodation, especially those who wanted to share with other guests to save money. However, this put additional stress on us and it was unpleasant to ask the guests for money for the bookings. In hindsight, it would have been better to send guests information regarding the venue area, websites they could use to book accommodation and a list of accommodation options, along with other guests' contacts.

Key takeaway

Reserve a special place for your wedding night!

Transportation

Plan your journey to the destination country and venue thoroughly and have backup transport options.

Why is it important?

Wedding transportation needs to be planned or arranged at the destination country for journeys to and from airports/train stations to your accommodation and the wedding venue to avoid disruptions.

Steps to take

Discuss with your partner about the type of vehicle (if any) you'd like to hire for the wedding. Give the vehicle hire company emergency contact numbers in case they need help with directions on the day. If feasible, you could borrow a nice car from a guest or a local and spruce it up with pretty decorations as well!

Questions to think about

* What transport options are there from your residence to your accommodation at the destination? How do they compare in terms of cost, time, comfort, availability and reviews?

   _____

* Can the venue hosts guide you regarding local transport options?

   _____

* Do you need to hire any vehicles for the guests?

   _____

* Would you like to book a limousine, luxury car, vintage car, horse and carriage, boat or helicopter or use your own car for your arrival and departure on the wedding day?

   _____

* What type, size and color of vehicle would you like?

---

* If it is cheaper, would you prefer a pickup and drop-off service for the wedding day instead of paying by the hour?

---

* Could you pre-book vehicles and get written confirmation regarding rental duration, prices, overtime fees, pickup and drop-off locations, dates, times and cancellation policies?

---

* Does the vehicle hire company have an operating license and insurance?

---

* Who pays for gas or mileage?

---

* Are decorations allowed on the rented vehicle?

My experience

We used online maps to plan our journey to our destination. Our flight arrival time was late at night, so we pre-booked a taxi from a company with good reviews. We sent guests a list of affordable transport options and a travel guide in advance. We also created groups on messenger apps and email chains for guests who would be arriving on the same date and at roughly the same time, so they could travel together to the venue area. Some of them became good friends afterwards! The wedding venue was located close to most people's accommodation so we didn't arrange any transport on the wedding day.

Key takeaway

Clarifying what vehicles you'll be getting and who will pay for transportation will enable you to stick to your budget and share bills fairly.

Wedding Insurance

Getting wedding insurance cover is entirely optional and depends on the risks and financial costs of rearranging your wedding, but travel insurance is a must.

Why is it important?

Wedding insurance can protect you from losses due to unforeseen events beyond your control and help you recover some of your wedding expenses. A good rule of thumb is to insure purchases that you cannot afford to lose.

Steps to take

While travel insurance with medical cover is a must, buying wedding insurance depends on your circumstances. If the costs of rearranging your wedding are quite high, then you can consider buying wedding insurance. Use a comparison website before choosing a provider. Read the terms and conditions to clarify what is covered. Keep a copy of the insurance contract page with contact and policy numbers so you can reach the provider quickly if needed. Have agreements with vendors in writing if possible and keep receipts for products and services and records of pending payments in case you need to make a claim later on.

Questions to think about

* How big is the risk and financial consequences of venue cancellation or bankruptcy, vendor service failure or last minute cancellations and risk of illnesses or accidents?

* How big is the risk of financial loss or damage related to expensive items like rings, wedding attire or gifts?

* Will the insurance cover cancellations due to personal reasons, financial difficulties or bad weather?

My experience

As our pre-paid wedding-related deposits and travel expenses were low, we decided to buy only travel insurance for any medical emergencies.

Key takeaway

Get travel insurance to ensure you are covered for any emergencies at the destination, including medical ones, even if you don't opt for wedding insurance.

Save the Date

MARIE + MARO
— May 25 —

Wedding Invitations

Digital wedding invitations can look great and save time and money. Customize them with memorable photos or designs inspired by your wedding vision or color scheme.

Why is it important?

Your guests may need to know your wedding date well in advance to be able to take leave from work to attend. It is thus best to send Save the Date invites as soon as your date and destination are confirmed. You can send another invitation closer to the wedding date once all the key bits of your wedding are finalized.

Steps to take

Consider sending email invites instead of paper ones and design them using online templates. To save on paper invites, use a normal printer and paper. Avoid bulky and layered paper invites to save on postage — use flat cards instead. Include an email address and phone number instead of RSVP cards and envelopes.

Questions to think about

* Would you like the invitations to be made by a specialist designer or yourself (e.g., using specialized websites)?

  _____

* If opting for a designer, can they provide invitation samples showcasing their previous work?

  _____

* Do you want to send both Save the Dates and wedding invites?

  _____

* Would you like to send printed or digital invitations or a mix of the two?

_____

* Would you like a formal, graphic, floral, minimal, vintage or casual style for your invitations?

_____

* Which fonts (e.g., calligraphy) and colors would you prefer and would you like them to match the wedding theme, if any?

_____

* Would you like to send any other information with the Save the Dates such as travel info like maps or directions so that guests can decide if it's a feasible trip for them?

_____

* What other information such as wedding details and dress code (black tie optional or invited/encouraged) do you need to add to the final invites once guests confirm attendance?

_____

* How many invitations do you need to send per family or couple and what is the cost of printing invites and postage?

_____

An invitation example:

Ms. Anna O'Sullivan and Mr. Ewan Smith are getting married! They would love to have you at their wedding ceremony and reception to celebrate their marriage on Sunday, the 2nd of June 2023, at 11 o' clock in the morning.

Location: Bellevue Resort, Corfu, Greece
Please RSVP by April 30, 2023

_anna_and_ewan@wedding.com_
15 Skyrock Hill, Edinburgh, EH1 2NG

My experience

We created electronic Save the Date invitations with our photo and included the wedding date, city and when to RSVP by (in about a month's time). No further details were provided as we hadn't finalized the venue by then.

We designed the final invitation based on our color scheme (the colors of hydrangea flowers) and included the venue details and timeline of the wedding day. These were sent to guests via email or messenger services, which was convenient, cheap, time-saving and better for the environment! We got quick responses too. We didn't have time to create a wedding website or blog. Alternatively, you can send out paper or wooden invites, which can become lovely keepsakes for the guests.

Key takeaway

Send out invitations to the guests you want most at the wedding as soon you have the date and venue fixed. Give them enough time to respond — best to let them know unofficially right at the start of your wedding planning!

Bridesmaids & Groomsmen

To avoid drama, ask your most supportive and adaptable friends to be your bridesmaids and groomsmen, not necessarily your closest friends!

Why is it important?

Bridesmaids and groomsmen advise and support the bride and groom respectively on wedding-related matters. Groomsmen run errands, usher guests to their seats (unless separate ushers are present), hold rings and help with transporting gifts. Bridesmaids and groomsmen also answer any wedding-related queries for the guests. You may also have flower girls and page boys who smile and scatter flower petals while looking cute.

Steps to take

Together with your partner, think about which friends would be most able to help you with wedding details. Do not ask someone to be your bridesmaid or groomsman out of courtesy or just because you were their bridesmaid or groomsman – you can always get them involved in other ways.

"Firing" a bridesmaid or a groomsman should only be a last resort option – if it threatens your relationship with the person or adversely affects your mental health. If it comes to it, reimburse any money spent by them and explain your decision gently over a meal or drink. To reduce wedding party-related costs, have one maid of honor and one best man. You have the ultimate say in how bridesmaids and groomsmen play a role in your wedding!

Questions to think about

* Would you like to have a wedding party with any or all of the following: best man, maid of honor, bridesmaids, groomsmen, ushers, flower girls, ring bearers, altar or page boys?

---

* How much commitment do you need from them? Could you put them in charge of various tasks for efficiency?

---

* Will you buy their outfits or will they do this themselves? Who will pay for them? If on a limited budget, be upfront about it.

---

* Would you like the colors and styles of the bridesmaids' dresses to match the wedding theme or color scheme or venue background or would you like to opt for mismatched bridesmaid dresses?

---

* Do the chosen outfits fit everyone or do you need any alterations?

---

* Can the wedding party formalwear be rented or pre-worn?

---

* Will the bridesmaids carry bouquets and will the groomsmen wear boutonnieres (flowers worn in a buttonhole) matching the bridesmaids' bouquet styles?

---

* Would you like your bridesmaids and groomsmen to throw lavish bachelor/bachelorette parties, casual ones like a BBQ at a friend's place or a local park, or nothing at all?

---

* Will you take your wedding party out for drinks etc., to thank them?

My experience

My fiancé had asked a close friend to be his best man and I'd asked four of my friends to be my bridesmaids. One day, we went shopping for bridesmaid dresses with a couple of them. Then arose a dilemma – one of the other bridesmaids lived in another country and wanted to select her own dress. So we decided to match the color and style rather than have the same dress for everyone. But getting a consensus was close to impossible. This didn't help, especially as I hadn't found my own dress at the time.

I thus decided against the idea of having bridesmaids altogether. As I had more friends who could have also been my bridesmaids, I was happy in the end as no one would feel left out. Although not everything went according to plan, in retrospect, it proved to be the right decision and everyone had a good time at the wedding.

Key takeaway

When it comes to choosing your bridesmaids and groomsmen, follow your instincts!

The Wedding Dress

The bride needs to feel comfortable as well as beautiful in her wedding dress. If you are truly happy with a dress, don't let it go!

Why is it important?

The image of the traditional bridal dress has evolved over centuries. In the modern Western tradition, it is typically a white dress, as shown in movies. However, fashion is ever-changing and wedding dresses may be of various kinds and colors.

Steps to take

Think about what style of dress makes you happy and start searching for it.

Questions to think about

* What is your budget for the wedding dress, including alterations? Remember that you may only wear it once!

_____

* Would you prefer an A-line, mermaid or trumpet, vintage, bohemian, ball gown or sheath style of wedding dress? Check online for pictures.

_____

* Size-wise: would you like it short, long, midi or mini? For color: white, cream, mono-colored, multi-colored or patterned? Plain or embroidered or jeweled? With or without a veil? Neckline style: strapless, sweetheart, off-shoulder, halter or scoop?

_____

* What kind of accessories will look good with your dress? Would you like special lingerie, stockings, shoes, gloves, a purse, a wrap or jewelry?

_____

* For religious wedding sites, do you need to wear a wrap or bolero for strapless gowns?

_____

* Are there specialist bridal or retail clothing stores in your area or can you order online to try on dresses? Are there stores where you can find designer outfits for less?

_____

* Are there any second-hand or thrift or charity shops where you can buy or rent a wedding dress at a low price?

_____

* Can you ask a trusted person to accompany you for trial fittings at off-peak hours as the store will be less busy and get his or her honest opinion about how you look in various dresses?

_____

* Does your dress height and style look fine with your shoes or do you need some alterations? Bridal shoes need not be expensive as they likely won't be visible under your wedding dress.

_____

* Do you have any backup outfits for emergencies?

_____

My experience

I wanted a white/off-white embroidered and sparkly full-length bridal dress with a slight flare. I tried to look for my dress online but was unable to find anything I liked. I then visited a few bridal stores but unfortunately, I had no luck finding a suitable dress. I'd almost given up hope of finding a dress when an unexpected breakthrough happened. My search coincided with a holiday in Barcelona with some friends. It was in a small family-run bridal store that I almost walked past where I found my dress!

It was an unforgettably breathtaking moment. It was the dress of my dreams — an ex-display jeweled dress being sold for a third of the price! However, my friends cautioned against making an impulsive purchase and I had the inevitable thought of 'What if there's something better out there?', so I let it go.

I spent the next few weekends looking for and trying on dresses in various stores back home but couldn't stop thinking about the dress in Barcelona. Luckily, I had taken the store's business card and emailed them to ask about the dress. They advised me to visit and see if they still had it. I went back hoping against hope – the dress was still available! I tried it on and felt happy instantly. It felt like *it was meant to be*.

Key takeaway

The search for an ideal dress may overwhelm you, but don't be disheartened. You *will* find your dress. The key is to feel happy and pretty in whatever you choose.

The Groom's Attire

The groom needs to be comfortable yet look distinctively stylish. Consider renting the groom's attire if it will be seldom used.

Why is it important?

The groom's attire needs to enable the groom to stand out from the other guests and also be compatible with the bride's overall look.

Steps to take

Try out a few outfits before you choose one — ensure a good fit and comfort. If possible, buy a nice suit you can reuse in the future or just rent the vest and tie if you'd like to wear a suit that you already own.

Questions to think about

* What's your budget for the groom's attire including alterations? Would you be fine with wearing non-designer black tuxedos or ordinary suits to save money?

  _____

* Can you rent a tux or suit instead of buying, or buy from charity or thrift stores? Average rentals in the US are around $150–$185.

  _____

* Which of the following items would you need: tuxedo, suit, tie, vest, bow tie, shirt, cummerbund, suspenders, shoes, socks and cufflinks?

  _____

* How comfortable and fitting is your attire while walking, standing or sitting down? For instance, the suit jacket's arms should not exceed one's fingertips, the suit shouldn't be so tight on the chest that the buttons could pop, squatting should be possible without

  splitting seams and lifting arms should be comfortably achieved to at least just below shoulder height.

---

* Will there be enough time for any required alterations? Note that rentals cannot be altered. If shoulder and armholes do not fit, it is better to change jacket size than alter these.

---

* Do you have backup suits in case of any emergencies ?

---

* Will groomsmen need to match their suits to the groom or have their own unique matching or non-matching styles?

---

* Will groomsmen pay for their own rentals or suit purchases?

My experience

As may be expected, finding the groom's attire turned out to be far easier than buying my wedding dress. We started by visiting local men's formalwear stores where my fiancé tried out a few suits in various colors and styles. Luckily, we found some stylish and reasonably priced suits that would fit my tall fiancé. He chose a suit that could also be worn on other formal occasions. We then visited a local tailor to check the fit and he suggested several changes. In the end, all the alterations were carried out within a few days. The whole process was much more relaxed than shopping for the bridal dress!

Key takeaway

When it comes to the groom's attire, style, comfort and cost are the three main considerations.

Hair & Makeup

Have a hair and makeup trial before the wedding day to avoid unpleasant surprises. Choose a style that makes you feel good!

Why is it important?

Bridal hair styling and makeup can significantly embellish a bride's overall look. This can be done by someone you know or professionally.

Steps to take

It is worth spending some time to find the right hairstylist and makeup artist for you as it will help you feel confident and beautiful on the big day.

Questions to think about

* Can you begin a self-care regimen including exercising, eating nutritious food, and skin and hair treatments a few weeks before the wedding to look and feel good?

* Would you like to go for a natural, retro, glamorous or bold look?

* Would you like to have a chignon or natural flowing curls or waves or short hairstyles?

* How will your hair and makeup appear in natural light and in photographs?

* Can the venue hosts recommend any hairstylists and makeup artists or do you know anyone who can do your hair and makeup?

* How much will the hairstylists and makeup artists charge and how much time can they devote to you at a trial and on the wedding day?

_____

* Can you ask a friend or relative who does good hair and makeup to help on the day in case of emergencies?

_____

* Do you want your hairstylist to use fresh flowers instead of a veil?

_____

My experience

Wanting to look my best on the wedding day, I decided to have a hair and makeup trial session prior to the wedding with a professional hairstylist and a makeup artist. I'd searched online for local hairstylists and makeup artists in Greece and ended up with a shortlist of around 10 people after looking at their portfolios and reviews. I asked them about their rates and availability. Once I made my choice, I booked a trial a couple of days before the wedding. I took my own makeup kit for hygiene reasons and hair accessories like combs and pins.

The trial turned out to be very important. After the session, I couldn't recognize myself in the mirror and the look didn't really match my personality. I then requested a couple of friends who did good makeup themselves to accompany me on the wedding day during the makeup session. They guided the same makeup artist to go for a far more natural style than she had envisioned. I was happier with the final look. I hadn't had time for any skin or hair treatments, but in the hands of the talented professionals, this turned out not to be an issue at all.

Key takeaway

With the help of a good hairstylist and makeup artist, you can look your best on your wedding day.

Wedding Rings

Get cheaper backup replica rings to wear during any activities where your rings could get lost or damaged.

Why is it important?

Exchanging rings is traditional in Western weddings but is becoming more common in other cultures. You don't have to buy expensive rings just because others do so. To learn some interesting facts about diamond rings, check out the video: Why Engagement Rings Are a Scam – Adam Ruins Everything https://www.youtube.com/watch?v=N5kWuiifBGU.

Steps to take

Discuss with your partner about what rings mean for you both and how much of the budget you'd like to allocate to them. Grab rings at a bargain from antique stores or online.

Questions to think about

* Do you want to exchange rings at your wedding?

---

* What do rings signify to you and your partner?

---

* What is your budget for rings? Can you buy rings online, locally or in places you travel to during the wedding planning period?

---

* Do you prefer rings that are plain, ornate, have embedded gems or are tailor-made?

---

* Would you like similar or different colors and styles of rings for you and your partner?

  _____

* What material and color would you like your rings to be? For instance: white gold, yellow gold, rose gold, silver, graphite or titanium colored.

  _____

* Would you like any inscriptions engraved on the rings?

  _____

* Do you need to purchase any insurance for the rings (if they too expensive to lose)?

  _____

My experience

The idea of having rings at a wedding ceremony is ingrained in our culture today. Be it in movies or books, the image of a wedding is closely associated with the exchange of rings. However, we didn't want to spend an exorbitant amount on rings. For us, wearing rings would simply broadcast our marriage and bond to others.

So we started by visiting various local jewelry stores to check out their ring collections. I wanted to wear a silver ring but once I tried a few samples on, I realized that a rose gold color would suit my skin tone better. This immediately narrowed down our options. I found a ring which was rose gold with subtle sparkling gems. For my fiancé, we bought a matching rose gold ring without any embellishments. We also purchased similar looking rings for ourselves for about $15 each (the originals were about $400 each) to wear during trips or activities like swimming where we could potentially lose our rings.

Key takeaway

Have wedding rings if it symbolizes your commitment and love to one another as a couple and display it to others. Otherwise, you can skip it or opt for creative alternatives.

The Wedding Ceremony

Ease of combining the legal ceremony with the social wedding depends on the destination wedding laws and the time available to sort out necessary paperwork.

Why is it important?

There are two parts to the wedding ceremony: legal and social. The legal part ensures that the wedding is solemnized before the law while the social part involves celebrating with family and friends. If you have separate legal and social ceremonies, you can invite a small circle of family and friends to the legal ceremony or hold it in private with only the two of you.

Steps to take

Traditional Western ceremonies start with the bride's entrance (see next chapter), followed by the bridal party walking down the aisle and the groom waiting at the altar. The officiant welcomes the couple and there might be a song or hymn. The officiant explains the vows that the couple are about to take and asks if there's any reason that they should not marry. Then vows are exchanged. Certain words may be mandatory but one's own vows could also be added. The best man then hands the wedding rings to the officiant and the couple places them in each other's ring finger (not legally required). Following this, the officiant officially pronounces the couple to be married and says that they may kiss.

Religious ceremonies may have some religious readings, prayers, a sermon and songs at this point. Depending on the country, the marriage license may need to be signed next in the presence of witnesses. The ceremony ends with closing words from the officiant and the couple exiting, followed by the wedding party and guests. You can adapt any of the above steps for yourselves.

Questions to think about

* Would you like to combine the legal marriage ceremony with the social wedding blessing or separate the two?

* What are the local laws for a civil ceremony and is your planned ceremony legally binding? Do you need any witnesses to sign your marriage license?

* What type of ceremony would you like to have: traditional, civil or alternative?

* If you want a religious ceremony, have you considered the rules regarding ceremony structure, people, location and your religious affiliations?

* What would be the location, order and duration of your ceremony?

* Will your guests be seated or standing during the ceremony? Will there be seats for people who can't stand for long?

* Would you like to exchange wedding vows and will they be officiant-led or personalized?

* Will there be any readings, poetry, songs or hymns?

* Will there be any cultural traditions or symbolic act such as the exchange of rings?

* Will the bride be escorted by someone or arrive alone?

  _____

* How do you wish to conclude the ceremony?

  _____

* Do you wish to have an alternative ceremony such as a candle
  ceremony, sand ceremony or hand fasting?

  _____

My experience

When we decided on Greece as our wedding destination, we realized that we didn't have enough time to arrange the necessary paperwork for a legal wedding there. Hence, we got our marriage license in our country of residence and decided to have the social wedding in Greece. As soon as we found someone to officiate the Greek wedding, we requested him to have the wedding ceremony outdoors.

At the ceremony, my fiancé handed me my bouquet and we entered together (more details in the next chapter). The officiant then welcomed everyone and the ceremony commenced. He read out our vows and then the best man recited some verses on love which were translated into other languages for the benefit of some guests. We exchanged rings and the ceremony ended with me tossing my bouquet. One of my friends caught the bouquet and got married within a year!

Key takeaway

Your wedding ceremony is the most important part of your wedding day. It is where you make important promises to your beloved in front of everyone. You can share your background story about how you met and your shared hopes for your future during the ceremony to make it unique and personal.

Wedding Entrance & Exit

Your wedding entrance and exit can be customized to make your wedding more memorable and fun.

Why is it important?

The wedding entrance and exit are important to plan in order to ensure a smooth start and end to the ceremony. It also helps to organize the seating arrangements for the guests.

Steps to take

When planning your ceremony entrance and exit, there is no right or wrong; only consider what you and your partner would like.

Questions to think about

* Would you like a grand entrance and exit or a quieter walk down the aisle?

  _____

* If you prefer a grand entrance or exit, would you like a flash mob, to land in a helicopter, parachute or balloon, to arrive on a horse or by boat, do a stage curtain entrance, sing or dance your way in, use smoke effects, hire dancers or musicians, have a line dance with everyone, swap outfits, have a rose petal or confetti or balloon shower, bring pets, have fireworks or sparklers or even project videos or images such as your own silhouette?

  _____

* Will you enter and exit the ceremony accompanied by music?

  _____

* Will any songs/hymns be sung or played when you enter or exit? Will you prepare music sheets for guests if you want them to join in?

_____

* Do you need to make a music playlist for the prelude, processional and recessional?

_____

* On what device must any music be stored (check with the venue) and do you need a backup copy?

_____

My experience

I'd always envisaged a traditional bridal entrance. I would enter the ceremony from the back and walk towards the officiant and my fiancé. All guests would be gathered already, either seated or standing. The standard bridal entrance that you see in movies. The venue hostess however suggested something a bit more extravagant – she recommended that I arrive in a boat! As the ceremony venue was situated on the island's coast, it was almost a natural thing to do. Moreover, her family owned a boat and were happy to escort me in it.

And so, I came in a boat from a nearby mooring area, like a captain in a white dress in front of a steering wheel. The guests and the groom cheered upon my arrival, as I came into view from behind a hill. It was a bit scary initially since I was driving a boat for the very first time. But I got the hang of it pretty quickly and it became part of the amazing experience of the special day! Upon arrival, I walked up a long flight of stairs and entered the ceremony area with my fiancé, accompanied by Pachelbel's Canon in D Major. We exited together to an adjacent area to chat with our guests after the ceremony.

Key takeaway

Think of your dream wedding and venue structure to plan your entrance and exit from the ceremony.

Wedding Photos & Videos

Choose your photographer and videographer well, as wedding photos and videos will enable you to relive your wedding for years to come.

Why is it important?

Your wedding photos and videos will enhance the precious recollections of your special day. You can also share these with those who cannot attend your wedding day.

Steps to take

When deciding on a photographer, check if their sample images are out of focus or over-exposed and whether the people in the photos look relaxed and natural. For videos, look for sound quality, image focus, lighting and type of music used. Ask that the photographer and videographer coordinate their shots. Request the highest possible resolutions for any shots and videos with 300 pixels per inch as a minimum. Opt for a digital package and make your own prints later.

Trust your chosen professionals to take the right shots and do their job well – giving them freedom to choose their shots can help leverage their skills better. Ask guests to take photos and upload them via apps or file sharing services. Have prizes for the best photo and video!

Questions to think about

* Would you like to hire a professional photographer and a videographer or would you like someone you know to take your wedding photos and videos?

* Would you like a photojournalistic (capturing the day's events like a story), formal, glamorous, candid, creative or vintage style for photos, and documentary or cinematic styles for videos? Would you like photos in color and/or black-and-white?

---

* Can your chosen photographer suggest a good videographer or vice-versa?

---

* Would you like to capture the wedding preparations, ceremony, group shots, wedding party shots, couple-only shots and the reception?

---

* For videos, would you like full ceremony footage, speeches and toasts, shorter highlights (10 minutes) and/or a trailer video (1–3 minutes)?

---

* Have you discussed timings, duration, accommodation, travel, photo and video delivery times, fees including deposit and taxes and equipment needed with the professionals?

---

* Do you need to communicate the photographer's and videographer's arrival times to their accommodation at the destination or venue in advance?

Example initial email to contact photographer/videographer:

Hello,

I would like to ask about your availability to photograph (videograph) our wedding in Corfu on June 2, 2023. Our ceremony will be held outdoors during late afternoon (3:00 pm).

We are a couple in our late twenties and we liked your style of photography (videography) very much. It would be lovely to have a few shots of the groom and bride preparations, the ceremony, some romantic couple-only

*shots, family and friends' photos with the couple including a group photo
with all guests and the reception. Would you please let us know your fees
including taxes and share your wedding portfolio?*

Looking forward to hearing from you.

*Kind regards,
Mona Lisa*

My experience

Right from the onset, we decided that wedding photography and
videography were the non-negotiables for us in terms of quality and
expense. We treated this as a long term investment as photos and
videos would make the wedding come alive long after the day was over.
Our online search was rather productive and we found several
professionals in Greece.

The styles that they adopted were wide-ranging — some had overly
processed photos and videos or special effects, others preferred a more
natural style, while some others were more experimental with colors
and exposure. We carefully looked through all the portfolios and
selected a few that we admired. In addition, we asked a couple of
amateur photographer friends to take a look at the portfolios to get
more of an expert opinion. We wrote to the shortlisted professionals,
asking for their availability and fees.

Finally, we chose a photographer, a videographer, as well as a drone
photographer. Coincidentally, the photographer and videographer
turned out to be friends! We spoke about desired photo and video
styles, number of photos and video length, the overall day's timeline,
travel and accommodation. Once we agreed on all the terms, we paid
for fuel expenses, accommodation and a 20% deposit. We also had a
photo booth with props so guests could take spontaneous fun selfies.

We made full payment when we received the photos and videos, a
month after the wedding. They turned out to be beautiful with just the
right amount of editing. For the drone photos, we made full payment
in advance. Getting hold of these was challenging as the photographer
was not as responsive afterwards, so never make full payment upfront!

Key takeaway

Depending on priorities, wedding photos and videos may be quite high on your list. If you can afford it, hire professionals to capture the memories of your special day so you can treasure them forever.

Decorations

DIY decorations can personalize your ceremony and reception settings and are a fun way to get guests involved as well as save money.

Why is it important?

Decorations can significantly boost the beauty of your venue and influence the wedding day ambiance.

Steps to take

Think about your ideal wedding vision to start planning what decorations you'd like. To save, create personalized table decorations or have bigger tables as they need fewer centerpieces and tablecloths. Buy flowers wholesale and arrange them in jars yourselves. You can also use tiny Christmas lights to add instant elegance to your venue. Beauty doesn't necessarily require extravagance!

Questions to think about

* Would you like decorations for both the ceremony and reception?

   _____

* What is your budget for decorations?

   _____

* Would you like to outsource the setup of decorations or do some DIY decorating?

   _____

* Would you like the decorations to match your wedding theme or color scheme?

   _____

* Do you need any reception table decorations including linen and items like chairs, china, glasses and cutlery?

  _____

* Would you like to provide place cards or menus at the reception?

  _____

* Would you like to supply printed order of service sheets or programs?

  _____

* What fonts would you prefer for any printed material?

  _____

* What kind of ceremony and reception lighting would you like?

  _____

* Will you have sufficient space in your luggage to carry DIY decorations?

  _____

My experience

As we had a beautiful ceremony background, we did not need many decorations. To match the venue's ambiance, we chose the colors of hydrangea flowers as our color scheme. These colors blended really well with the sea and mountains in the background. We made pompoms, paper flowers and bought balloons and wooden hearts. We also brought accessories such as pins, tape, ribbons, pins and lace with us. In addition, we prepared beautifully designed place cards for the reception which we filled in with each guest's name. My fiancé also made origami decorations which we placed on each table. The caterers provided the rest of the decorations for the reception.

It rained unexpectedly in the morning of the wedding, so we had very little time to put up decorations. This was an additional responsibility for me on such a busy day. Several friends helped out in the final hour to decorate and this became an opportunity for guests to get to know each other better! In hindsight, we should've asked specific people to be in charge of decorations to make the process more organized.

Key takeaway

The beauty of a destination wedding is that you don't need many decorations. Whether you get married on a beach, surrounded by white sand and palm trees, or in a lush garden setting, the scenery can serve as a naturally beautiful backdrop, significantly cutting costs.

Flowers

Use flowers to make your wedding background look even more stunning or to beautify less ornate settings.

Why is it important?

Use of flowers can be symbolic. Flowers enhance the beauty of a venue with their look and smell. Artificial flowers that resemble real ones could be a money-saving alternative. Although they are not wonderfully fragrant, they can be reused afterwards and do not trigger allergies.

Steps to take

Ask a florist for suggestions on floral arrangements by showing a photo of your dress and the venue. Be flexible so that your florist can choose the most affordable flowers for you. You can also buy flowers from a local market and make floral arrangements yourself. You can add fruits and vegetables to flowers as well. You can use real in-season flowers for bridal bouquets and artificial silk ones for the rest. Call the florist a day or two before the wedding to ensure timely preparation of your order and clarify the delivery procedure and the accessories supplied. Having your wedding on dates other than Valentine's Day and special holidays may reduce your floral expenses.

Questions to think about

* Would you like to have flowers for the wedding ceremony, reception as well as the rehearsal dinner?

* For the ceremony, would you like to have bouquets for yourself as well as your bridesmaids and groomsmen (for buttonholes and corsages), flower girls and family members and flower petals for guests to toss on you?

* Do you need flowers for general decorations such as entrances, a ceremonial arch and tables?

* Would you like the floral styles (e.g., ornate, bold, beachy, rustic, quirky, minimalist) at the venue to complement the bride's bouquet, dress, wedding theme or color scheme?

* For the reception, would you like flowers on each table?

* Would you like to have fresh or artificial flowers or a mix of both?

* Would you like similar flowers in a bunch (all white or pastels or colorful hues) or of mixed types and colors?

* Do you need any other décor items for flowers such as chair and table covers, aisle decorations, candles, pots, trellises or vases?

My experience

We got flowers for our ceremony from a local florist recommended by the venue hosts. The florist showed us different types of floral arrangements in bouquets and hanging pots. We selected two pretty pots to hang from the trees surrounding the ceremony area and a colorful bouquet for myself. I'd also bought several artificial flower bouquets matching our color scheme as a backup. We ended up using them to decorate the perimeter of the ceremony site. On the wedding day, the venue hosts collected the flowers from the florist, which helped us very much.

Key takeaway

Use floral arrangements to uplift your spirits and fulfill your wedding vision.

Catering

Plan a menu such that it makes your reception uniquely memorable and delegate the finer food and drink details to the catering team.

Why is it important?

Catering is important as tasty food forms a key part of your guests' experience of the day and keeps energy levels up and spirits high.

Steps to take

Embrace local cuisine and drinks to save and incorporate destination flavors. Opt for well-loved menu items instead of fancy food. To save on beverages, bring out one signature drink for toasts and switch to less expensive options like wine and beer after.

Questions to think about

* Does the venue have in-house caterers or know food suppliers?

_____

* How will the catering prices influence the total guest count — do menu costs differ between adults and children?

_____

* Are the prices flat-rate or per item on the menu and are waiters included in the costs?

_____

* Will you limit the number of free drinks and make subsequent drinks available for purchase? Can guests bring their own drinks?

_____

* How many courses including dessert and after dinner drinks would you like? Will you serve only appetizers and cocktails at the reception? Would you like to have snacks and canapés for your guests while they are mingling before dinner?

_____

* Would you like to have local specialties or your favorite foods or menu items from your first date or proposal or a collection of world foods to impress your guests?

_____

* Would you like to have your wedding cake as dessert? If you'd like ice-cream, will there be a cooling and storage facility for it?

_____

* Would you like the chef to cook in front of the guests?

_____

* Do any guests have allergies and dietary restrictions that need to be communicated to the venue and caterers?

_____

* By when do you need to confirm guest numbers to the caterers?

_____

* Who will provide cutlery, dinnerware, tables and chairs?

_____

* Will the tables contain name cards and menus?

_____

* How will guests enter the reception area and when? Will guests need to queue and will someone lead the guests to their tables?

_____

* Would you like food to be served as a sit down dinner with a seating plan, a buffet, or something different like a BBQ or have food trucks? Will guests change tables between courses to encourage mingling?

_____

My experience

It was difficult to find information on caterers in Corfu due to their limited presence online. As we didn't understand the local language, we felt it wise to let the venue arrange the catering. We selected menu items after consulting a Greek friend. The catering team got back to us about what was feasible within the limited time frame and budget.

We had Greek food for our mains and baklava and ice-cream for dessert. The food was novel to us while being tasty, fresh and filling. It was served as a buffet but people could still sit down and eat as they wanted. This ensured easy mingling among guests without being chaotic. Afterwards, the venue hosts distributed any excess food to their resort residents to enjoy. Everyone was happy and full by the end of the evening.

Key takeaway

Prioritize your and your partner's tastes when it comes to the menu and don't try to please all your guests.

Cakes

Time the cake cutting to ensure that guests are happy and full of energy.

Why is it important?

The wedding cake can be an unforgettable part of the wedding experience. However, it is not essential.

Steps to take

Choose a cake with your partner based on both of your tastes. You can have cupcakes or a square wedding cake to serve easily to guests. You can also decorate your cake with fruits or flowers.

Questions to think about

* Will the reception caterers supply the cake or can they or the venue hosts suggest local bakers?

  _____

* What budget would you like to allocate to the cake and is there any extra fee involved for cake delivery, cutting or serving?

  _____

* How many cake tiers would you need (three tiers would likely serve 100 guests)?

  _____

* How big should the portion sizes be and can people take second helpings?

  _____

* Would you like to have a traditional or an innovative cake (like a stack of brownies topped with ice cream)?

_____

* What would you both prefer for the cake flavors and can you go for a tasting session?

_____

* Would you like the cake design (including toppers) to match your wedding theme, style or be something meaningful to you?

_____

* Do any of your guests have allergies or special dietary requirements?

_____

* Do you need refrigeration to store or space to assemble the cake?

_____

* When would you like to cut the cake (e.g., during dessert or between the ceremony and reception)?

_____

* Can you coordinate with the decorators or caterers to match the shape and linen of the serving table to that of the cake?

_____

My experience

I wanted to have a chocolate cake that would taste delicious but I didn't have any preference for the design. The venue organizers suggested that we leave the details for them to arrange with the caterers and together, they came up with the design and flavors. It turned out to be the best cake most of us had ever tasted and looked really grand!

We decided to cut the cake right after the ceremony to ensure guests didn't get hungry until the reception dinner. The venue hosts distributed any leftover cake to their residents and everyone enjoyed it very much. In hindsight, we could have saved a bit of the cake and dessert for the following day's brunch!

Key takeaway

Having a wedding cake is tradition but think about what you and your partner want. You can go without one if your budget doesn't permit or serve it as a dessert to save.

Entertainment

Have a range of activities for guests of all ages to enjoy so that they have fun-filled memories of the day.

Why is it important?

Wedding entertainment depends on the couple's tastes and budget. It helps to make the reception memorable and enjoyable for all.

Steps to take

Think about what kind of entertainment will make you and your partner feel happy. But don't forget your younger and older guests. If possible, perform a survey beforehand to understand your guests' tastes but remember that you can't please everyone.

Questions to think about

* What kind of entertainment would you like and for when? Ideas include: live music, dance, karaoke, flash mob, disco, fireworks, comedy, having a magician or caricaturist, games, awards for best dressed guests, quizzes, piñatas and scavenger hunts.

* What is your entertainment budget?

* How many forms of entertainment would you like to have?

* Do the venue organizers have any entertainment suggestions?

* Can you get written agreements with rates including overtime and cancellation policies before booking any entertainment?

---

* Would you like guests to prepare a surprise for you such as a funny speech, play, performance or a movie? If yes, what audio-visual equipment would be needed?

---

* Would you like to continue celebrating with an after-party and extended celebrations the following day?

Music & Dance

* Do you want to have live performers or a DJ who plays recorded music? The latter would usually be cheaper.

---

* Would you like to have musicians or vocalists?

---

* Do the venue hosts know a list of local performers?

---

* Are there reviews or audio/video samples of the performers to help check quality, stage presence, interaction with crowd, guests' reactions and smoothness of transitions between performances?

---

* Would you like pop, rock, metal, jazz, swing, country, classical music or dance?

---

* What should be the sequence and length of the performances?

---

* What space, equipment (e.g., tables, chairs, stands, mics or amplifiers) and setup time do the performers or the DJ require?

---

* For recorded music, is there a playlist of songs you can prepare for the DJ? Are there any songs you *don't* want played?

_____

* Do you have a backup storage device with playlists?

_____

* Would you like music to be played during the reception meal?

_____

* Would you like to do a first dance? If yes, is there a song that has special meaning to you as a couple?

_____

My experience

We had informally asked each guest in advance what their favorite song was. Using this information, we created a reception playlist for the DJ, whom we found via the venue hosts. Everyone was thrilled! Following the hosts' suggestion, we had local dancers who performed Greek dances and conducted group dances with all our guests. We then danced to the DJ's mix of songs for the rest of the evening. Fireworks were popular in local venues but would have exceeded our budget.

Key takeaway

Tailor the wedding entertainment to your and your partner's tastes first and then consider your guests but be mindful of your budget.

Speeches & Toasts

Wedding speeches and toasts may seem daunting but can make your wedding extra memorable and fun!

Why is it important?

Speeches and toasts in Western weddings are traditionally made at the reception, before or after the meal or during intervals between courses. Speeches are typically made by the bride's father, the groom, the best man, the bride and the maid of honor. They generally involve thanking guests and sharing anecdotes about the bride and groom so that guests get a unique perspective on the couple.

Steps to take

* Don't let just anyone give a speech or toast and have a maximum of 5 speeches (5–10 minutes each) so as not to bore guests.
* Start by thanking everyone for sharing your special day with you, with special mentions for people who helped put the wedding together.
* Make a list of your partner's endearing qualities and think of a funny or special shared experience to talk about. Reminisce about how you met, how you fell in love and how much your partner means to you. End on a positive note with a vision of your future together.
* Include an appropriate funny story about each other as a couple in your speech to make it entertaining and memorable. But don't make the speech too funny as it may backfire!
* Don't say anything that might offend anyone present and do not mention any exes.
* Write down the speech and bring notes in case you blank out but don't read from them.
* Practice with a friend or in front of the mirror to feel more confident.

Questions to think about

*   Would you like to have speeches and toasts at your wedding?

  _____

*   Who would you like to give speeches or toasts?

  _____

*   Is there a special story about your partner that you'd like to share during the toasts?

  _____

*   Are there any guests who don't speak the language and would need a translated printout of your speech or toast?

  _____

My experience

As we had limited time, we decided to skip speeches and toasts at the reception due to the additional worry of preparing these. Moreover, some of the guests didn't speak English and could feel left out.

Key takeaway

An alternative to speeches could be to recite poems, sing songs or have a couple's quiz to keep everyone engaged.

Wedding Favors

Use favors to thank your guests and remind them of your wedding in a personalized way.

Why is it important?

Favors comprising sugared almonds were traditionally given to guests at some European weddings to signify blessings or good luck. Nowadays, favors are used to thank guests for attending a wedding. Wedding favors are wide-ranging, from personalized, useful, fun, quirky keepsake items to something delicious and consumable.

Steps to take

Ideas for favors include chocolates, sweets, teabags, soaps, lotions, lip balms, oils, scented candles, seeds, exotic succulents, puzzle pieces, brain teaser games, socks, flip flops, sunglasses, tote bags, jars, drinks glasses, bottle openers, coasters, place mats, matchboxes, mini lanterns, fridge magnets, luggage tags, hand fans, polaroid photos, photo frames, badges, notebooks, books, engraved pencils and rubber stamps. You can make wedding favors with friends or skip them altogether if you are on a tight budget.

Questions to think about

* Would you like to give wedding favors to your guests at the wedding or send thank you cards afterwards?

  _____

* How much of your budget would you like to allocate to favors?

  _____

* Would you like to create the wedding favors yourselves?

  _____

* Would you like to give favors linked to your wedding theme, like jars with jam for rustic themes or polaroid shots for vintage ones?

_____

* Is the climate at the venue suitable for the favors (e.g., chocolate might melt in intense heat)?

_____

* Would any items containing glass or liquids be allowed during the journey back or be easy for guests to carry home?

_____

* Would you like to distribute favors while welcoming guests, with place cards at the reception, after dinner or before they leave?

_____

My experience

We wanted to send each guest a personalized wedding photo taken with them individually at the wedding as a token of thanks. I then came across a suggestion to consider donating to charities like WaterAid instead of giving typical wedding favors. This inspired us to buy beautiful handmade items as favors from a charity which helps children from Eastern European orphanages to build their own lives. We also gave guests personalized place cards which we'd designed and photos taken with them at the wedding afterwards.

Key takeaway

Wedding favors are completely optional and can be items that reflect your tastes or personality. Be creative and you can come up with inexpensive yet thoughtful gifts.

Wedding Gifts

Ask guests to send any gifts directly to your home address to avoid carrying them around at the destination or during your honeymoon.

Why is it important?

Wedding gifts are traditionally given to help the couple start their new life together and are expected to help recover some of the wedding expenses. However, gift giving at destination weddings may not be dictated by usual wedding etiquette — making the effort to travel and attend may be considered sufficient in itself due to the costs involved.

Steps to take

If you are concerned about your guests' expenses, you can offset their costs by not creating a gift registry as their presence is sufficient. Communicate this clearly so guests know exactly what to expect. Otherwise, you may wish to create a gift registry or a fund for your honeymoon and share it with your guests. This would contain a list of items that you wish to receive on the occasion of your wedding. This can also be linked to a website which is used to communicate wedding information to guests. Let your guests know about your registry as soon as you have a list ready. Take down your gift registry a few months after the wedding.

Questions to think about

* Would you like to get any wedding gifts from guests?

_____

* Would you prefer cash, gift cards, donations to a charity, specific items listed in a gift registry or leave it to your guests to make their own choices?

_____

* How will you transport your gifts home?

* If making a gift registry, what do you need for your long-term future together?

* Is there a variety of items with a wide range of price points on your gift registry?

* Do the stores, if any, on your gift registry have return policies?

My experience

We had asked our guests not to bring any wedding gifts as we knew that it was a significant expense to attend the wedding for the majority of our guests. But a few guests still brought us gifts such as kitchen items and gift cards.

Key takeaway

Communication with guests is key with respect to gifts. Record who gives what and thank them as soon as possible.

Gifts for One Another

Consider selecting a gift such as an unforgettable shared experience (e.g., holiday, cruise, hiking, hot air balloon ride, horse-riding) to create more life-long memories!

Why is it important?

Giving your partner a wedding gift, material or otherwise, might be an additional way to celebrate your bond with one another.

Steps to take

Buy wedding gifts for your partner only if it makes you happy or if you feel your partner will appreciate it. Your partner may also be expecting a gift (you know best!), so it might be a good idea to be prepared. Just don't leave the purchase until the last minute!

Questions to think about

* Do you normally give your partner gifts on special occasions?

  _____

* Do gifts make your partner genuinely happy?

  _____

My experience

I wasn't expecting a wedding gift from my husband. But during our honeymoon, I received a big surprise – my husband had bought a beautiful delicate necklace for me! He chose a moment when I was least expecting it and this added to the surprise. His gesture of taking up the daunting task of visiting various stores and selecting the gift carefully made me truly happy. I hadn't gotten him any gifts but had booked special meals and tours for our honeymoon as a surprise.

Key takeaway

Buy a wedding gift for your partner if you think it's going to make them happy — you know your partner best!

Wedding Rehearsal

Send everyone attending the wedding rehearsal an outline of the ceremony timeline in advance.

Why is it important?

Wedding rehearsals typically include the wedding party, close family members and the officiant. Rehearsals help to ensure a smooth entrance, exit, guest seating and the ceremony itself.

Steps to take

The rehearsal should be a quick affair (20 minutes maximum) and relaxed. Have a family BBQ for your rehearsal dinner or skip it altogether if you have a tight budget. Rehearsals are entirely optional.

Questions to think about

* Do you have an assertive and organized guest who could take charge of the rehearsal as well as the wedding day's timeline?

  _____

* Would you like to have a rehearsal dinner following the rehearsal?

  _____

The rehearsal sequence is entirely dependent on your wedding type but could resemble the following:

* Ask everyone to stand where they would during the ceremony. Briefly go through the ceremony, noting when events like the exchange of rings or lighting of candles will take place. If any guest is reading a passage, song or verse, send them the text in advance.
* Practice walking in and out with enough space maintained between the couple and guests. Let guests know where to meet

after exiting.

* Practice the entrance following the exit — the officiant, groom, best man and groomsmen enter first in traditional weddings. Next come the family, the parents of the groom and the mother of the bride. Finally, the bridesmaids, maid of honor and flower girl enter. After all guests are in place, the bride enters typically with her escort (typically the bride's father), accompanied by music.

* Once the bride reaches the front, the bride's escort congratulates her, gives her a kiss and shakes the groom's hand. The bride then hands her bouquet to the maid of honor and steps forward beside the groom, while the escort goes to where they will be seated. The bride and groom then face each other and hold hands in front of the officiant. The maid of honor checks the bride's dress and train and then the ceremony proceeds.

My experience

We decided against having a wedding rehearsal as time was tight during the days leading up to the wedding and there were still many things to take care of. In retrospect, a rehearsal might have made us a bit more comfortable with various aspects of the actual ceremony. In particular, it could have made the entrance and exit for the couple and the guests a bit more organized.

Key takeaway

A wedding rehearsal can help you be more prepared and feel more confident about your wedding day.

Wedding Day Timeline

Don't attempt to time wedding day activities perfectly but have enough time between events for any eventualities or delays to enable seamless transitions.

Why is it important?

The goal of the wedding day timeline is to construct a timetable with the timing and sequence of the day's activities to ensure that things go as planned, as far as possible.

Steps to take

Events often take longer than expected, so it's best to allow extra time for them. An example timeline is shown at the end of this chapter.

Questions to think about

* What will be the ceremony and reception times? Consider the availability of your officiant, the venue and the local climate.

  _____

* When should your guests arrive?

  _____

* How will the number of guests influence the day's activities and times?

  _____

* What will be the duration of the ceremony and subsequent celebrations?

  _____

* How much time will you need for photos (group and couple-only shots)?

  _____

* How much time should you allot for transport between the wedding ceremony and reception venues if they are separate?

_____

* When will food, drinks or aperitifs be served?

_____

* How much time will there be for entertainment and is there a time limit for ending the celebrations?

_____

* Can someone be in charge on the day to monitor timelines so you don't worry about this?

_____

* Will you share the wedding day timeline in advance with guests?

_____

My experience

Once we had the wedding date fixed, we started deciding on the day's timeline. The venue hosts suggested starting the ceremony at 3:00pm as temperatures would be cooler and the summer sun less intense. Hosting the ceremony and reception at the same venue saved us valuable time. The hosts were very relaxed, so guests could arrive at any time and get a drink. Most guests arrived 30–60 minutes before the start of the ceremony. The ceremony lasted about 40 minutes including the bridal entrance.

Afterwards, people came to congratulate us, followed by drinks and cake. Leaving the guests to mingle freely, we headed out to a nearby beach for a photoshoot, which took about an hour. We returned to the venue for dinner, which was followed by a party. The celebrations officially ended around midnight. After dismantling some decorations, we headed to a beach to chat and swim with friends.

Key takeaway

Have easy transitions between events so you and your guests find it relaxing to switch to the next event.

Wedding Day Timeline

08:00 AM	Breakfast
09:00 AM	Hair and makeup
09:30 AM	Decorations set up
10:00 AM	Get dressed
12:00 PM	Lunch
01:00 PM	Travel to venue
02:45 PM	Bride arrives
03:00 PM	Ceremony begins
04:00 PM	Ceremony ends with bouquet toss
04:30 PM	Cake cutting
05:00 PM	Photo session
06:00 PM	Drinks & canapés
06:45 PM	Reception begins
07:00 PM	Dinner
07:30 PM	Speeches & Toasts
07:50 PM	Dessert
08:30 PM	First dance
09:00 PM	Party!
11:30 PM	Guests depart

The Day After

Consider having a rough plan for meals, trips and other activities for the day after the wedding so you can relax and enjoy the day.

Why is it important?

The day after the wedding is often forgotten during the planning. However, having an idea about the day's activities can help greatly if you are not going for your honeymoon right after the wedding.

Steps to take

Request friends and family to help clean up after the wedding to make it more fun as well as avoid cleaning fees.

Questions to think about

* Are there any remaining bills still to be paid before you leave the destination?

  _____

* Who is responsible for cleaning up after the wedding and by when does it need to be done?

  _____

* Would you like to save some souvenirs from the wedding such as the bride's bouquet, place cards or decorations? If yes, could you ask specific people to take care of this?

  _____

* Would you like to book an informal brunch or dinner in advance for the day after, especially if other guests are expected to join, or would you prefer to play it by ear?

  _____

* Would you like to go somewhere the following day by yourselves or with friends and family?

  _____

* Would you like to spend quality time with your family and friends before they leave?

  _____

My experience

We hadn't given the day after the wedding a second thought during the wedding preparations. We decided last minute to have drinks and snacks at the venue with some friends. Afterwards, we took down all remaining decorations. It was fun and relaxing to tidy up with friends amidst the beautiful awe-inspiring landscape! We then went out for sightseeing with guests who still remained. Having a rough idea of the locations to visit helped with organizing the day's activities for such a large group. We had delicious Greek food for brunch and later that evening, we dined at the venue. The meal was wonderful and full of free treats!

Key takeaway

The important thing is to relax the day after the wedding — you have made it through an unforgettable event with people closest to you and are now with the love of your life!

Post-wedding Tasks

Have a to-do list for post-wedding tasks so you can finish them timely and calmly.

Why is it important?

Keeping track of post-wedding tasks will help you be less stressed once the big event is over.

Steps to take

Think about all the tasks you need to complete after the wedding and make a list with your partner.

Questions to think about

* Do you have to return any rented items?

_____

* Are there any outstanding wedding-related bills to settle?

_____

* Would you like to clean and preserve your wedding attire?

_____

* Would you like to donate or sell your wedding attire?

_____

* Do you need to go through your decorations or gifts from the wedding and decide whether to give some away?

_____

* Are there any gifts that need to be exchanged or returned or any gift cards to be used by their expiry date?

_____

* Would you like to send out personalized emails with photos from the wedding or thank you cards to guests?

  _____

* When would you like to stop hosting your wedding website or take down your gift registry if you have any?

  _____

* Would you or your partner or both like to legally change your surnames?

  _____

* Would you like to write any reviews related to your wedding vendors?

  _____

My experience

After the wedding, we sent thank you cards to all guests digitally and gave each guest printed photos taken with them at the wedding. We also sent thank you notes to the officiant and venue hosts and reviewed our service providers as a thank you. We then requested our photos and videos from the professionals. We went through the photos and printed the best ones for our wedding album. We also asked all our guests to share their photos from the wedding on a website so we could download them all from one place.

Later, I carefully stored my wedding dress for a couple of close friends to wear in the future. We re-used some of the decorations for other events or passed them on to friends. Next, we paid any outstanding bills and performed calculations to estimate the total wedding costs. Lastly, I legally changed my surname and updated my name for various accounts and services and for any upcoming bookings.

Key takeaway

Planning post-wedding tasks in advance helps relieve stress after the big day and enables you to stay organized.

Packing

Pack efficiently for both the wedding and honeymoon to save time and effort during the trip.

Why is it important?

Packing in advance can help you avoid forgetting something vital and any related stress and negative consequences.

Steps to take

* Consider minimizing the number of items you take with you as they can be inconvenient to manage and heavy to carry from one location to another.
* Pack items in sections according to categories such as everyday clothing, laundry bag, wedding apparel, shoes, accessories, decorations, etc.
* Pack items efficiently by rolling clothes and so on. Watch online videos for tips on how to fold clothes compactly.
* Have a couple of outfits including spare underwear and socks, essentials like medicines, documents, phones, power adapters and device chargers and expensive items like wedding attire, rings and cameras with memory cards in your hand luggage in case of emergencies such as luggage delays or losses.
* For hot climates, pack swimwear, appropriate outdoor wear, sandals, sunscreen, insect sprays, sunglasses and perfume or deodorant. For colder places, carry winter wear like gloves, hat, scarves, hand and feet warmers, body cream and warm socks.
* If traveling in winter from a colder climate to a warmer one and there is a risk of dragging a lot of heavy winter stuff around, consider asking a guest to carry your winter coat or collect you from the airport.
* Take an emergency kit with medicines, first aid and beauty accessories for yourselves and your guests.

* Request guests to send gifts directly to your home address to avoid shipping or carrying them home. Keep extra space in your luggage for gifts just in case.

Questions to think about

* How many clothing and other items do you and your partner normally need when you go on holidays?

_____

* Do you have any guests you could ask to carry some of your stuff?

_____

My experience

We were experienced in packing efficiently and had learned to take minimum luggage with us on trips the hard way. We thus carefully considered what to take and packed only essentials as we had limited space and didn't want to carry heavy suitcases to the destination. We maintained separate sections for wedding and honeymoon items in two suitcases. All documents, rings and emergency medicines along with our camera and wedding attire were packed in our carry-on luggage as these would be too expensive to lose. Our checked baggage consisted mostly of decorations and clothing items.

We had asked guests not to bring any gifts, although a couple of friends still brought some. These luckily fit into the available luggage space we had but was pretty heavy to carry around, especially during our honeymoon. In hindsight, sending some luggage back home through a guest would have been really helpful (a really excellent wedding gift for guests to offer!).

Key takeaway

Be savvy and make a list as early as possible and pack only what you need. Begin the packing process as soon as you are able to so that you can purchase any necessary items that are missing well in advance.

The Honeymoon

Why is it important?

Planning your honeymoon can be the most relaxing part of your wedding planning journey! But your honeymoon needs to be arranged well as it is about quality time with your beloved.

Steps to take

Plan your honeymoon with your partner like you would plan a really relaxing holiday. On days like Tuesdays and Wednesdays, purchase your transport and accommodation in your maiden names. Travel midweek to get cheaper rates. Look for deals or last minute discounts as well. Collect air miles and travel rewards if you can. If you plan your honeymoon right after the wedding, arrange to send any excess luggage home. Take local currency, ATM cards, photo IDs, passports, visas, cameras with memory cards, adapters or converters, medication, toiletries and weather-appropriate clothing with you as well as translation and map apps or books. Lastly, learn about the local tipping culture beforehand.

Questions to think about

* What is your honeymoon budget?

_____

* Would you like a city break, exotic island visit, luxury resort relaxation, forest fun, sporty or wilder adventures, cozy countryside getaway or a cruise experience for your honeymoon?

_____

* Would you like a mini-moon or a longer honeymoon?

_____

* Would you like to go for your honeymoon right after the wedding, the following day or sometime later due to better vacation options or nicer climates in your dream destination?

_____

* Would you like to choose your honeymoon destination primarily based on accessibility from the wedding location, weather, activity choices, accommodation options (deluxe resort, all-inclusive, B&B) or travel and accommodation costs?

_____

* Could you consult someone who's been to the honeymoon destination you are considering or watch videos to get a feel for the place before you book the trip?

_____

* Do you need visas or any vaccinations for your honeymoon destination?

_____

* Would you like to book any of the key logistics in advance like airport transfers, lounge access for layovers, excursions, transfers to and from a remote island, special meals, rental cars, cruises or couple's massages or would you prefer a completely spontaneous experience and get someone else (e.g., Pack Up + Go) to plan your honeymoon in a surprise destination for you?

_____

My experience

We wanted to spend our honeymoon in a warm and scenic place. As we would already be in Greece for the wedding, we looked at places accessible from Corfu. We decided on Santorini due to lower flight costs. Due to our budget and time constraints, we could only afford a 4-day mini-moon. We stayed in Corfu for a day after the wedding, had a one-day stopover at Athens and then headed to Santorini. We properly planned the transport to and from the island; the rest of the honeymoon was pretty spontaneous! We booked a luxurious apartment for one day as a treat. We did lots of sightseeing, had great dinners and watched some breathtakingly glorious sunsets.

Key takeaway

Don't be influenced by other people's honeymoon stories or ideas – research your options and do what feels right for you as a couple. For example, make your honeymoon a road trip from your wedding location to save. Your honeymoon should provide much-needed relaxation and quality bonding time with your beloved. Enjoy it!

Top Tips

* Things don't have to be perfect.
* Things will not always turn out as expected but it all adds to the spontaneity and fun of your wedding day!
* Don't worry too much about the planning — things will be fine in the end.
* Take things one at a time and complete each task as best you can.
* Decide your wedding budget as early as you can.
* Ask friends and family to help you with various aspects of the wedding.
* Find someone to help you with language issues at the destination and to guide you with things like destination laws.
* Use the venue's network of vendors (florists, catering, etc.) if possible and ask the venue hosts for advice on various aspects of your wedding. This may save time and make it easier to organize the wedding from abroad.
* Choose local options (at the destination) for your wedding. This will save you money and also help bolster the local economy!
* Keep a contact list of all vendors with a record of payments due.
* Ask vendors to put in writing their rates, payments made, payments due and the services expected, whenever possible.
* Ensure all vendors and guests have the correct address and directions to the venue as well as your and your venue coordinator's contact numbers.
* Keep emergency contact numbers and emergency money with you for any unforeseen circumstances.
* Check local phone tariff options and purchase a suitable package for the duration of the wedding trip.
* Download apps for taxis or vehicle hires in advance.
* Keep extra copies of your passport (and visas, if relevant) and the address of your embassy closest to your destination with you in case your documents get stolen.
* Don't forget to buy travel insurance but remember that it may not cover unusual weather conditions.
* Keep backups of any important items such as playlists, seating

plans, special dietary requirements, etc., with you in case of emergencies.

* Check if your wedding attire fits properly as soon as possible to have enough time for alterations.

* Carry comfortable alternatives for shoes and underclothes with you.

* Plan well for a change in weather at your destination in terms of having appropriate sun or rain cover at the venue as well as wedding clothing and accessory choices.

* Optional events you could host include an engagement party, a bridal shower, Bachelor/Bachelorette parties, a welcome party and a bridesmaid luncheon.

* Pack efficiently with minimum stuff. Ask guests to send any gifts directly to your home address.

Your Wedding Checklist

Wedding Fundamentals

3-6 Months Earlier

- [ ] You're engaged!
- [ ] Get engagement photos if you wish.
- [ ] Decide your wedding style.
- [ ] Set a maximum budget.
- [ ] Choose a country.
- [ ] Sort out marriage paperwork.
- [ ] Get a marriage license (if separating civil and social ceremonies).
- [ ] Decide on the time of year and select the wedding date.
- [ ] Make a guest list and inform people close to you informally.
- [ ] Send Save the Date cards to potential guests.
- [ ] Research, contact and reserve ceremony and reception venues.
- [ ] Find a ceremony officiant and book.
- [ ] Reserve accommodation for the duration of your stay: before and after the wedding and for the wedding night.
- [ ] Arrange transportation for the wedding day and for your travels before and after the wedding day.
- [ ] Get travel and wedding insurance if required.
- [ ] Send invitations to guests with gift expectations.

Wedding Attire

- [ ] Select your best man, maid of honor, bridesmaids, groomsmen, ushers, flower girls, altar or page boys (as desired).
- [ ] Start shopping for a wedding dress, tuxedo or suit, shoes and accessories.

2-3 Months Earlier

- [ ] Plan and shop for bridesmaids' and groomsmen's outfits and other wedding party members if needed.
- [ ] Find and book makeup artist and hairstylist.
- [ ] Shop for and buy wedding rings.

Wedding Ceremony

- [ ] Plan the format of the ceremony along with readings and vows.
- [ ] Ask relevant people to prepare readings and speeches.
- [ ] Choose the exact location for the ceremony within the venue.
- [ ] Plan wedding entrance and exit along with ceremony music.
- [ ] Research and book wedding photographer and videographer.

Wedding Reception

- [ ] Book caterers and decide on the menu.
- [ ] Choose and order the wedding cake.

1-2 Months Earlier

Wedding Decorations

- [ ] Buy decorations.
- [ ] Design place cards and order of service sheets.
- [ ] Find a florist and order flowers.

Wedding Reception (Continued)

- [ ] Book your wedding entertainment.
- [ ] Write speeches and ask relevant people to prepare them in advance.
- [ ] Finalize your guest list, decide on a seating plan and share this with the venue and caterers.

Wedding Gifts

- [ ] Purchase gifts or favors for guests and/or the wedding party.
- [ ] Share your gift registry with guests if you have one.
- [ ] Buy a wedding gift for your partner (if you wish).

Final Pre-Wedding Tasks

- [ ] Arrange a wedding rehearsal.
- [ ] Decide the wedding day timeline.
- [ ] Let the venue and vendors such as caterers know exact guest numbers along with dietary requirements.
- [ ] Organize activities like brunch for the day after, if relevant.
- [ ] Decide what to pack for flight and trip and pack in separate bags or sections.
- [ ] Have a final dress fitting.
- [ ] Book your honeymoon.
- [ ] Send the final wedding day timeline to guests.
- [ ] Attend Bachelor/Bachelorette parties.
- [ ] Confirm parking arrangements at the venue for the big day.
- [ ] Travel to the destination.
- [ ] Have hair and makeup trials.
- [ ] Attend wedding rehearsal and rehearsal dinner.
- [ ] Stay hydrated.
- [ ] Arrange wedding attire for the big day.
- [ ] Sleep early.
- [ ] Get married!

Post-Wedding Tasks

- [ ] Clean up. Save the bridal bouquet if you want. Arrange for any leftover food to be distributed or stored for the next day.
- [ ] Pay all vendors.
- [ ] Go on your honeymoon!

- ☐ Return any rented stuff or gifts if required.
- ☐ Clean the wedding gown and suit.
- ☐ Send thank you cards to guests and/or the venue hosts.
- ☐ Review vendors as a thank you (optional).
- ☐ Follow up with the photographer and the videographer on wedding photos and videos.
- ☐ Pat yourself on the back for organizing your dream wedding!
- ☐ Relax!

Acknowledgments

Writing this book would not have been possible without the support and encouragement of my husband, Igor. He stood by me through some really difficult times during the writing of this piece.

I am truly thankful to my friend Lieke, who happily read through the entire work and highlighted the good and bad aspects to bring my writing to life. She kept me going even when motivation was running low. I am very grateful to my friend Donna for all her constructive criticism and ideas — this book would not have been shaped the way it is now without her invaluable input. Special thanks to my friend Ti for all her thoughtful questions and comments — they helped ensure that what I wrote was logical and helpful.

A big thank you to my family for their encouragement throughout the production of this book. Finally, to all those friends who have been a part of my writing journey (you know who you are) — a very big thank you!

Printed in Great Britain
by Amazon